KAIZEN IN SCHOOLS

DR DHEERAJ MEHROTRA

Contents

Preface

Kaizen In Schools is a step towards improvement in school management. It shares and re-visits novel ways to promote quality learning and teaching as a priority.

The term KAIZEN is a Japanese word that activates continuous improvement and is hence a very important aspect of the teaching-learning process.

I am sure the book shall relate to KAIZEN as an opportunity to excel the learning within classrooms.

Dr Dheeraj Mehrotra

www.authordheerajmehrotra.com

ONE

KAIZEN IN SCHOOLS

♡♡♡

School buildings need to be under surveillance on a 24×7 basis. Assure your CCTV cameras are in working order with the pace of recording. A dimensional view of the recorded data should be analysed to ensure that the charges/ vice principal/ admin staff/ Principal/ Management are routine. The findings must be analysed and queried towards the students' interest in totality.

 PPP

Emergency exit plans must be in their place. Every floor must have an ENTRY and an EXIT plan on display. Check on locks and barricaders to settle the students with trained, armed guards on duty. Assure there is a public sign designating an official meeting point in the school. It can be called an assembly point; a meeting point is a fixed (safe) place where students can gather or report during an emergency or a fire drill etc.

PPP

Appoint Senior Students as FLOOR in charge of managing an easy flow of the traffic class wise during recess, before and after assembly, and getting over the school. Each floor must have a TEACHER on duty and must be housed with a small staff room occupied by teachers teaching on the respective floor of the classes. Any teacher having a free period must have an eye on the students moving out for any reason.

ⰅⰅⰅ

Preparing students to remain calm in case of attacks is how schools can ensure student safety.

This must be practised periodically through MOCK Drills. Ensure inclusive and equitable quality education and promote lifelong learning opportunities for all. The children should be given mock sessions to deal with situations like these and must not react but contribute to a safe exit without fear and anxiety.

ⰅⰅⰅ

Ragging and bullying must be checked regularly. Class Monitors must be coached to inform the Head of School of any such incident in private. Teachers need to be indisputable partners, the front-line actors whom the students trustingly turn to for advice, guidance, for inspiration as they stand on the threshold of young adulthood. The teachers should act like extended family members to the students.

ⵊⵊⵊ

Teachers need to govern their relationship with the students and their parents. They are monitored to be documented using the INTERACTION Register to promote safety as a PRIORITY. Parents need to submit a family photograph with the child in the centre to assure liaison and networking for safety and security reasons. This record contributes to knowing the family and the child better.

ⵊⵊⵊ

Schools should also appoint counsellors/ psychologists to help students address trauma/rage/depression issues. The objective should teach learners a set of values and a sense of moral responsibility and belong to the nation. The teacher understands the child better and can mould the child to the best format and requirements. Sound advice without AWE is a must for every student by the TEACHER.

ᐅᐅᐅ

Schools need to ensure that students can take care of themselves and tackle situations like abductions/abuse. Assure the spending of money on training people and equipping them with measures of checking CHILD ABUSE/ POCSO or The Protection of Children from Sexual Offences Act (POCSO Act). School management must ensure at least two workshops on CHILD ABUSE in every session.

ᐅᐅᐅ

Schools need to ensure that the food consumed by children on school premises (at the cafeteria or in a school mess) follows stringent measures and guidelines to maintain hygiene. Food served at schools must undergo regular quality checks to ensure that the food is fit for consumption.

ᗺᗺᗺ

Smartphone technology can be used to a school's advantage to maintain students' safety and security. Check for the research adoption of using BLOCKCHAIN Technology to protect students within the campus. The use of AI and Augmented Reality is also on the cards. Technology adoption is hence a requisite for running a school peacefully.

▷▷▷

Install EFFECTIVE CCTV Cameras in all Nooks and Corners of the School Premises, including the entry of the WASHROOMS and entry/ exit points of the school. It is suggested to be installed in every classroom, and the parents should be given access to the feed through a mobile phone app.

ᐅᐅᐅ

The School Compound Should Be Fenced and Gated. Guards should be on ROUND duty with proper LATHIS and TORCH with a whistle. The respective locations of these guards should be monitored using the GPRS tracking system.

ᐅᐅᐅ

There Should Be Security Personal Stationed at the School Gate and must MONITOR the CCTV Camera on the round. The Entry/ Exit REGISTER should be marked and duly signed regularly for ENTRY and EXIT.

ᐅᐅᐅ

Clearance Should Be Given to Any Visitor before Entering the School Premises by the person responsible for the MEETING. Teachers must stand guard in front of classroom doors, regularly watching for misconduct during the Parent/ Teacher Meetings.

ᐅᐅᐅ

Students and Workers Should Always Be In Possession of their ID cards and valid security IDs. Police officers need to be given the authority to conduct random pre-emptive searches of students' lockers and personal property. A check on driving licenses and vehicles needs to be monitored as well.

ᐅᐅᐅ

Proper Security Check Must Be Conducted Before Employing Teachers and Other Employees. Schools must conduct periodic criminal history checks of school employees during their employment. In addition, the school must establish policies requiring school employees to report any arrests for crimes to their school employees within 24 hours of such arrests.

ᐅᐅᐅ

Students Should Be Trained On Security Related Subjects/ incidences/ scenario. The school must be a place in practice where students develop both socially and emotionally. Staff members and the students should know WHAT TO DO IN A CRISIS? There has to be a collaboration with the POLICE.

ᐅᐅᐅ

A Leadership Team and a Security Club Should Be Formed in the School with REGULAR safety and security guidelines. The team should include all types of individuals from the school, community and others. These individuals should develop school-wide prevention plans, analyse the needs assessment, and formulate short and long-term goals.

▷▷▷

Only the Parents of Students or Someone Duly Assigned Should Be Allowed to Pickup Students from the School. Staff must be trained to recognise the parents, and their training ensures understanding, support and use of a school-wide violence prevention plan. The constant movement makes the students and the faculty comfortable with the crisis plan.

▷▷▷

Central Security Alarm Should Be Installed in the School Premises. A mock drill for the same must be carried out from time to time. There has to be a complete 360 degree integrated security solution from intrusion detection security systems, video surveillance and fire alarm test and inspections to mass notification, emergency communication, an indication of any Terrorist Attack and everything in between.

❦❦❦

Students' Bags Should Be Searched from Time to Time to Prevent Them from Bringing Dangerous Weapons into the School. These random searches must be based on unique, school-wide needs to ensure school safety and should be truly random. A random search can not be done to target any individual child in the school.

ꝗꝗꝗ

Students' Activities should be strictly monitored to prevent them from Joining Secret Cults. Individual traits of the children need to be monitored, and constant positive reinforcement and motivation need to be given. This is possible only if the child feels connected to the Teacher. Monitoring activates the possibility for classroom development.

ꝗꝗꝗ

Students Should Be Encouraged To Report any Suspicious Moves or Persons within the School Premises to the School Management. Teachers should connect with other teachers that interact with the child in the next grade and help work on the child's developmental process. We must provide various reporting options like anonymous reporting strategies through websites, text, phones and designated teachers, counsellors and peers on priority.

ÞÞÞ

Students Should Only Be Allowed To Leave the School Premises Only When They Have a Pass from the Security Post. No child should be allowed to walk home without prior consent from a parent or guardian. Parents must understand that it is their responsibility of theirs' and not the school's once their children have left the school premises.

ÞÞÞ

People Should Be Discouraged from Loitering or Parking Their Cars outside the School fence. *The schools should encourage parents to adopt the carpool system to drop and pick up their children. This may reduce traffic chaos outside schools and ease the flow of vehicles. The priority is to gel with the society/ public/ neighbourhood injunction for ease of business and transit within the framework of security.*

ᢒᢒᢒ

The use of mobile phones in school settings or environments is a topic of debate. **Students Should Not Be Allowed to Make Use of Mobile Phones within the School Premises.** *There should not be any BLANKET Ban on phones, but when in emergencies, the children should be allowed to use them. They should only have access to a mobile phone where there is a need to contact parents/ guardians in an emergency.*

ᢒᢒᢒ

Students and PARENTS Should Be Issued Access Cards with the BIO-METRIC system

and recognition. This system can be used to purchase food and drink in the dining hall and use the library to manage the loan of books and submission of books issued earlier using the recognition.

ϷϷϷ

Kids Should Be Taught Not to Talk to Strangers within or even outside the school campus. The unfortunate incidents of abductions and molestations in and outside the schools with our students make it more important to educate our kids about Mr Danger Stranger and how and why they should continue to be vigilant all their life.

ϷϷϷ

Teach teachers To Be Vigilant on issues related to CYBER Bullying, CHILD Abuse and Racism. The child Abuse Identification and Reporting workshop is essential. The Child Abuse Identification & Reporting Workshop must be a priority for both the PARENTS and the Faculty.

ᕼᕼᕼ

Teach the school's emergency procedures via YOUTUBE Videos/ Simulation Games/ Mock Drills as a part of the ROUTINE exercise. Children should know how to respond to any EMERGENCY. Online drills sessions must be during SUPW periods in standard as an exercise in practice.

ᗺᗺᗺ

Teach the Travel Routes to and from the school for nearby locations. POICE and relief/ help/ emergency numbers must be landmarked and earmarked at every nook and corner of the school around the campus, and children and staff should be proactive for any assistance.

ϸϸϸ

All stakeholders need to be well-versed in school security and safety measures. A regular orientation towards any new building and exit and entry plans should be mentioned via exclusive videos and manuals to all the stakeholders to face any emergency.

ϸϸϸ

Overall, the environment is the most significant enabler of learning. It can be created by focuthreesing on three major components- the teachers, the technologies and the curriculum. Teacher Training is the critical component of the Finland model, along with the creative and customised curriculum. The "one size fits all" Indian education system, and rote memory-based exam only produces parrots, not creative thinkers.

ⱶⱶⱶ

***Staff** must be informed periodically on Student Safety and Behavioural Issues. The teachers should not limit their interaction with a class for a year but track the development of the children as they move on. The whole teaching and learning process should be immersed in a "facilitating" environment that is not easy to create. Just look at the home environment. It is all about control and command. This is where our children get started. Hence home, school environment and social values have to be in sync to produce the Finland system.*

ⱶⱶⱶ

***Any Loose Electrical Wires** must be tended to immediately. The admin/ staff/ prefect/ member of the student council on floor duty must inform the concerned authority of any* *short circuit or loose wiring on the campus of any kind.*

ᑭᑭᑭ

Regular structural audits must be conducted of the school building. There has to be a timely inspection of FIRE ALARMS/ FIRE FIGHTING equipment to be in place and in working order to handle any emergency. This must be tested via MOCK Drills on and off.

ᑭᑭᑭ

The Schools must ensure the railings and pathways are sturdy along the staircase and corridors. They must be well lit and guarded by an Adult during dispersal. Wherever practical, separate access points should be provided for people and vehicles to ensure the safe flow to and from the school boundary. From the fencing around its perimeter to the main entrance gates, visitors get a clear impression of a school's commitment to safety and security before entering its grounds.

ᗰᗰᗰ

Toilets at school ensure privacy and safety. Going to a school lacking proper basic facilities, like toilets, could be one of the most frustrating situations for many hence the entrance to the TOILETS needs to be monitored. Every student's move around the un-manned/ restricted places must be observed and checked using the CCTV Camera.

ᗰᗰᗰ

School ID cards are intended to identify the elementary, high school, or college students to prove their membership in the school or college. Badges and name tags must be mandatory for the TEACHING and NON-TEACHING STAFF. Assure meeting up of the SOCIAL and EMOTIONAL needs of the children through PEP talk and interactions and may include HOME VISITS by the teachers.

ᗰᗰᗰ

Police Verification of the Teaching and Non-Teaching Staff should always be undertaken. This may include checking the stakeholders' cultural and Parental Background of the stakeholders too as documented information. Ensuring employment of support staff only from authorised agencies and maintaining proper records is another one of the guidelines.

❥❥❥

CBSE Quote

"Schools must get the psychometric evaluation done for all the staff. Such verification and evaluation for non-teaching teams -such as bus drivers, conductors, peons and other support staff -may be done carefully. In a detailed manner," Psychometric Evaluation of the Teaching and Non-Teaching Staff should always be undertaken.

ϷϷϷ

The playground should be aesthetically designed and maintained regularly with opportunities for multi courts and games with physical activities. Assure every child's attendance to be marked thrice a day and messages sent to parents if their children are absent. Assure No child should be punished in such a way that could cause mental or physical trauma.

ϷϷϷ

The classrooms must be aesthetically designed with equipped ICT facilities and support mechanisms. Regularly update licenses for the software in use with proper anti-virus and a check on CYBER bullying with FIREWALLS installed in systems.

ᐳᐳᐳ

A check on having enough TOILETS separately for girls and boys/ Male and Female Staff, safe drinking water, medical room and counselling room. Among the preventive measures suggested for girls' safety are separate washrooms for boys and girls, at a suitable distance, and the deployment of a female attendant in the girls' bathroom.

ᐳᐳᐳ

All the students must be given Psychiatric Support and Counselling, particularly on Cyber Bullying. School counsellors should teach sex education classes, provide information to students about bullying and offer seminars on study skills. They MUST

collaborate with the teachers, parents and special educators to create a healthy learning environment that makes them feel comfortable.

ᑭᑭᑭ

Busses should follow clear mandates, including the seat to student ratio, display of emergency numbers, and tracking system. A female teacher or attendant should accompany a girl if she must leave the school for an exam or another event, and the school bus female attendant should not leave the bus unless the last girls are dropped to their destination.

ᑭᑭᑭ

Aesthetically designed furniture should be age-appropriate in classrooms at different levels. The school building should be prepared for natural light and ventilation inflow.

ᑭᑭᑭ

A school safety committee should be constituted to ensure and monitor safety practices. Student Council should be directed to shoulder the additional responsibility for the safety and security of the students. The school must also have a vigilance committee comprising parents, and the schools should follow it.

ᐅᐅᐅ

Visit the Police Station by the school's kids to understand the role of police in our daily lives and their contribution to the safety and security of the country's citizens. Schools need to take cognisance of safety issues as per the guidelines set by the boards and the government.

ᐅᐅᐅ

There has to be a regular METAL DETECTOR CHECK for Visitors. Assure school stakeholders are frequently trained to manage emergencies and disasters with good practice in conducting mock drills and evacuation drills.

Now at Amazon!

ᐳᐳᐳ

*There has to be a documented Safety Norm for every **LABORATORY** in the school. Check for the availability of facilities supporting differently-abled students. Students should never work in a science lab without their teachers. Students must be made to wear safety goggles, lab coats, and shoes in the science laboratory. In school science labs, loose clothes, sandals, and loose hair should be a strict **NO**.*

ᐳᐳᐳ

*Every student in the school and the teacher/ employee must know how to operate a fire fighting Equipment installed on the campus. Identify the **TWO** closest exits and all possible evacuation routes. Know locations of fire alarms and how to use them. Teachers and Students must report vandalised fire equipment to campus security.*

ᕈᕈᕈ

Regular Inspections of Fire Fighting Equipment must be on the cards. Assure stringent provisions for emergency management are in place for all types of FIRE and alarm during an emergency and call for nearest POLICE STATIONS and mention significant PHONE NUMBERS in place.

ᕈᕈᕈ

The Annual Curriculum plan of the school should integrate the academic, social, physical and emotional needs of the children. Identify what hazards are likely to affect the area in and around your school. Determine the severity of the impact of each identified hazard. Students and staff must be trained on using the plan and their responsibilities in a given response.

ᕈᕈᕈ

The infrastructure, including Computer Labs, Science Labs, and Math Labs, must be appropriate and meet expected standards ALL THE TIME. Areas, where students congregate while waiting for buses and associated pedestrian paths are adequate to avoid overcrowding. Access into each building is controllable through designated entry points. If possible, identify one entry point for visitors.

ԲԲԲ

The school must have adequate medical facilities and be equipped with a nurse/doctor to handle medical and other emergencies. Create at least one Administrator Emergency Tool Kit for each school building. Develop and distribute emergency response guides for each classroom. Establish and document procedures for providing students and staff access to mental health services.

ԲԲԲ

Restrooms, toilets, laboratory, playground, and classrooms must be CLEAN, AIRY, and WELL. Schools must also have ramps and need to admit students of disadvantaged groups and have SPECIAL Educators to assist the needy concerned. Send at least two girls/boys to the washroom at a time so that in case of an emergency, one of them can raise the alarm.

ᐅᐅᐅ

There should be separate TOILETS for Female and Male Staff. The school must also ensure adequate medical facilities and be equipped to handle medical and other emergencies. Without proper cleaning, washrooms can become breeding grounds for germs that can spread disease throughout the school population.

ᐅᐅᐅ

The Library should be airy and be equipped with an EMERGENCY Alarm System and Fire Fighting Equipment.

Use posters and bulletin boards to emphasise potential dangers and safety procedures.

Post legible, accurate emergency numbers and procedures.

ppp

The school must take the initiative to Conservation of Environment and take MAJOR initiatives in IMPLEMENTING Waste Management Practices. Use organic waste for composting and teach students about how it works. Schools can use the compost in the school gardens, saving on the cost of fertiliser and other chemicals. Schools could set up worm farms, which can be used to teach parts of the curriculum.

Now At Amazon

⊳⊳⊳

The school should have a provision for

***DIFFERENTLY ABLED INDIVIDUALS** should provide a conducive working environment with growth opportunities. Students in wheelchairs attend public schools more and more regularly. Schools must adhere to the norms for assistance to these children.*

ᐅᐅᐅ

There has to be a sense of SAFETY and SECURITY in the School, with regular evacuation drills being carried out from time to time.

Ref: Quote: Example

Fire Drill PM, #5 of 5, the School Year 2016-2017 3.21.17 @ 1:40 PM Evacuation/ Shelter Time: 1min, 00sec Participants: 45 total participants Drill Conducted by: Loretta Tobolske-Horn, Greenfield Principal Acknowledgement of Completed Drill: On File

at HCISD Office, 310 W. Bacon Street, Hillsdale

ᛞᛞᛞ

Schools Need an eye beyond CCTV Cameras.

A must check by teachers and knowing each child by the first name is very important. In addition, there has to be a HEALTH CARD for every child with all MEDICAL records in the count.

ᛞᛞᛞ

Schools must ensure all records in the school diary should be updated and recorded for easy reference. Parents must be communicated about their child's health issues, what so ever of PRIORITY.

"Nevertheless, no school can work well for children if parents and teachers do not act in

partnership on behalf of the children's best interests. Parents have every right to understand what is happening to their children at school, and teachers are responsible for sharing that......": - Dorothy Cohen.

ÞÞÞ

The schools should advocate, model, and teach safe, legal, and ethical use of digital information and technology; promote and model responsible social interaction related to technology and knowledge; celebrate Cyber Security Week and conduct activities to create awareness through cyber clubs.

ÞÞÞ

Check the Cyber Bullying, If any, through ONE on ONE interactions and observatory efforts. Frequent CYBER ethics sessions need to be observed and organised for the students, parents and other stakeholders. There has to be a digital technology program in places like

ERP which should serve as an interactive medium 'between the educators and the guardians."

ÞÞÞ

Check on CHILD ABUSE in practice by using friendly options with the students by asking them to share the uncomfortable moments they feel being around the school. It is up to us to ensure our children grow up in environments that build confidence, friendship, security, and happiness, irrespective of their family circumstances or backgrounds. Keeping children safe from harm requires a vigilant and informed community.

ÞÞÞ

Check on SECURITY agency people with their I-Cards, Lathis, Umbrella, Torch and Safety Belts. There has to be a fitness MEDICAL certificate available for all guards on duty.

ppp

Any water is logging in the washroom or around the washroom/ corridors.

A check is required on priority.

Well-designed school restrooms can enhance student health, deter misbehaviour, and conserve resources. The initiative should be that the children bring these behaviours home, thereby acting as agents of change in their communities.

ppp

Floors surfaces chipped or carpets in Music Rooms worn out with spots or holes may lead to sudden slipping of the children and this balancing. Safety precautions peculiar to any new lesson should be emphasised at the start of the class.

Available at Amazon

Observe if the Aisles are free of boxes, wastebaskets, chairs and other obstacles that may impede traffic within the campus. Check on the internal flooring of the classroom, lighting in the school, and the children are aware of the evacuation drill, and the classroom is naturally ventilated. Ideally, the classrooms must have rules towards letting the students set their climate of respect and responsibility.

ᐁᐁᐁ

Check on whether the doors have stoppers in classrooms. Students must check on their behaviours, and Teachers must help students correct their behaviours and help them understand violating the rules results in consequences. They should be told to respect ground rules, and the kids should feel free to discuss issues without fear.

ᐁᐁᐁ

Check on POWER sockets in classrooms, if any, that must be out of the reach of the children. Assure proper Earth wire towards protection against electric shock. The children should be told to stand clear of any fallen power lines. Remove unused wall outlets and apply tape over new plug holes or cord holders. Also, ensure they get dry when they come out of the swimming pools in the classrooms to operate computers or any electrical device in particular.

ᗡᗡᗡ

Five S in action with a special marking for FAN (F), and TUBE (T) as special mentions on switchboards within classrooms. A check update is required. 5S is a workplace organisation method that uses a list of five Japanese words: seiri, seitan, season, seiketsu, and shitsuke. These have been translated as "Sort", "Set In Order", "Shine", "Standardize," and "Sustain"

ᗡᗡᗡ

Evaluate the students' MEDICAL history from time to time, and teachers must study the child's health record as part of the routine. They must have a form of allergy, physical disability or if there is a cause or a case of bullying, with a keep of the information conveyed to the Head of the school and the Principal in the loop.

ᐅᐅᐅ

Are Staircases well lit?

"You can't study or learn if you don't feel safe at school."

—Bill Jenkins, director of Student Services,

Millard Public Schools (Omaha, Neb.)

The school MUST have an EMERGENCY plan A and B and MUST not be making decisions under DURESS that they have not practised.

"Students not only understand 'see something, say something,' but they also know who to tell and feel comfortable approaching them."

—Rex Barrett, acting director of security services, Prince George's County (Md.) Public Schools

ᚦᚦᚦ

Are Staircases free from litter, spills or clutter? Assure children travel on the right side of staircases and hallways. Appealing staircases will encourage use. The teachers and the charges must monitor slops and falls, sharp edges and the assurance of up to date maintenance.

ᚦᚦᚦ

Do Teachers or Students stand on some stand or ladders for teaching/ demonstrating supervision and support?. If need be, the assistance from students can be supported but under control. This is practical real-real learning and experience for them.

ᐳᐳᐳ

Do Students/ Teachers RUN in the area after assembly or during the getting over of the school?

A must check, and the solution is drawn for an easy and organised exit and entry to the assembly ground. The students should be guided during the dispersal. There has to be a public-address system to ensure timely and safe evacuation during an emergency.

ᐳᐳᐳ

Children should be briefed about safe touch and unsafe touch, avoiding interaction with strangers and reporting any and every concern, however irrelevant it may seem. Also, an average behaviour change has to be communicated to the parents. There has to be an open communication channel with the students, and they should be given a patient hearing for even the smallest of matters.

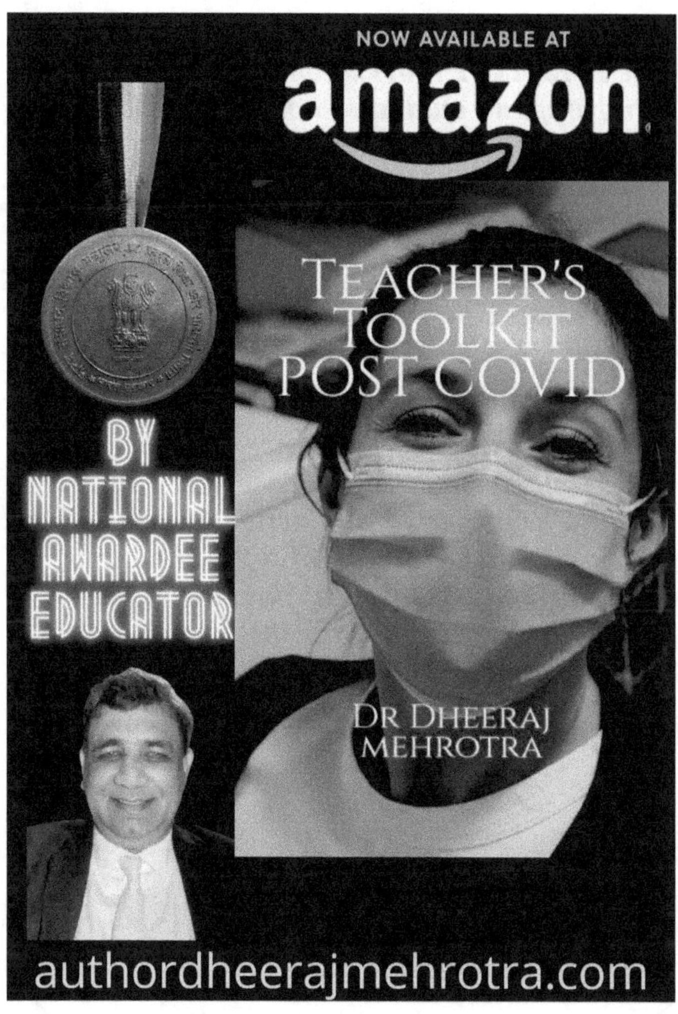

NOW AVAILABLE AT
amazon
TEACHER'S
TOOLKIT
POST COVID
BY
NATIONAL
AWARDEE
EDUCATOR
DR DHEERAJ
MEHROTRA
authordheerajmehrotra.com

➢➢➢

The buses and other school transport should be IDENTITY marked with helpline phone numbers, and students should be issued a Bus Badge with Bus Route Number. They should use only the allotted bus and bus stop. Boarding and alighting from the bus should be done in silence in an orderly manner.

ᗡᗡᗡ

Computers and SERVERS need supervision in LABS/ deserted rooms. Passwords and WIFI should be protected and activated timely for execution. Original Software should be preferred to assure attack of Malware or Virus in particular. Students should not be allowed to use external drives.

ᗡᗡᗡ

No Strangers should be allowed to Meet Children. No stranger, driver or family friend should be allowed to pick the children up. The Principals' helpline should be used to inform any irregularity. Students should not be allowed to drive motorised vehicles such as cars, scooters and motorcycles within or outside the school.

ᏢᏢᏢ

Do all employees know the exit locations and directions when in an EMERGENCY? EAP or Emergency Assembly Points should be located away from the building. Fire Exit Symbols should be in place for immediate evacuation using the nearest escape route. The schools must ENSURE School Building Level Emergency Preparedness and Response Plan.

ᏢᏢᏢ

Are fire drills conducted regularly? Check on Training of Task Forces, Demonstration, Mock Drills, develop emergency resource contact inventory for human resource, transport and tools required dealing with emergency response, Hazard Hunt Programmes, Training for First Aid Search and Rescue, and building evacuation drills regularly. It is recommended to prepare a detailed floor evacuation plan and conduct a mock exercise for an earthquake or a fire to test emergency plans and update the findings.

ᐳᐳᐳ

Assure a QUICK background check of visitors in the schools and information explored via IDs'. Involve PARENTS as partners in Safety and Security Mechanism in action. Assure Disaster Management in Education and formal training/workshops for all the stakeholders to mainstream the discipline of disaster risk management.

ᐳᐳᐳ

Are all incidents/ accidents adequately reported, investigated and documented? Check on provision to parents the information on school's emergency policies and procedures to further update on Emergency Notification Cards in the almanacks. The plans must execute as an EMERGENCY plan and keep the students safe when crisis strikes.

ϷϷϷ

Is medical help readily available? Assure procedure to evacuate the building, evacuate the premises, shift to temporary shelter, safeguard students and staff, notify parents, notify media, provide transportation and debrief procedures timely and appropriately. Make the vital PHONE numbers available in case of emergency to be painted on display around the campus.

ϷϷϷ

Enhancements. Employees need to be empowered to check and identify any uncommon person in safety. The school must appoint a PRO or a public information officer to provide information and the current status of the situation to the parents and other inquiring parties in case of an emergency.

ÞÞÞ

VISITORS Batch to be given to all who wish to come to the school during office hours. Also, ensure the emergency plans need to be reviewed and revised regularly. Make it a living document with modifications in a requisite timely. The document paperuld address prevention/ mitigation, preparedness, response and recovery aspects.

ÞÞÞ

Assure of conducting a preliminary assessment of preparedness measures of each school building. There has to be a review of the building layout and the surrounding areas for the evacuation of the students. Also, inspect equipment to ensure it operates during crises. Develop a command structure for responding to an emergency.

ÞÞÞ

Assure children walk on the side of the corridors to ensure everyone gets to classes safely. Make sure the good plans are never finished. They need to be constantly updated based on the experience, changing vulnerabilities, and assessing current capabilities. One must carry out shelter assessment needs for various situational responses. An emergency supply inventory should be checked and updated as per the expiry.

ppp

Assure children and any adult, RESPECT, if someone has an injury, excuse not to get in their way of walking. One must be aware and prepared; not being SCARED should be the priority. Every room in the school should have a map posted identifying two ways out. The exit paths should be obvious and kept free of obstruction.

ppp

Follow the rules to go up and down the stairs. Everyone safely exited the building; they should remain outside at a predetermined location until the 'all clear' green signal has been given to enter the installation again.

ϷϷϷ

Include TERRORISM THREAT in School Syllabi.

All schools up to the secondary level should include this as a very critical issue in their syllabi. It should be as compulsory for students as military service, which is mandatory for the youths in Israel. This is a security step towards safety and security scenscenarioshin schools.

ϷϷϷ

Assure and Make Sure there is a SILENCE ZONE in the school to monitor and assure discipline. Let the staff and students follow the same religion. Quiet Zones in schools and classrooms are an easy way to help meet a need that all students have at one time or another. The need to be able to take a break

from the noise and pressure of social interaction and recharge.

ÞÞÞ

Let the children play SMART and follow the elementary playground safely. Let the children follow for their turns in line. Assure attention by the teachers on swings, slides and other equipment. They must actively supervise students on playgrounds. Assure of age-appropriate playground equipment. The children should only be allowed in proper attire and choose playgrounds with shock-absorbing surfaces.

ÞÞÞ

Do you have a designated drop off and pick up area at your school? A defined pick up and drop points for walkers, bus takers and Parents' fetch & drop. The guided line-wise provision has to be a routine for average dispersal on all days and special requirements for the rainy/ emergency days accordingly. Specified Drop-off spots are locations near primary schools where parents can drop off or pick up their children.

ᗽᗽᗽ

Are safety rules displayed and visible?

**Check the updates on Step up for Students'
Health, promoting a healthy school
ecosystem. The schools need to provide a
monthly calendar for educating each child on
hygiene, nutrition, stress and vision through
educational videos and hands-on activities
integrated via guest lectures and workshops.**

TWO

KAIZEN THROUGH PARENTS' CONNECT

SMS', Groups via Whatsapp, FB Connect and Skype are some of the means to connect with the community of parents, the ultimate stakeholders of the learning community. The desire to know the updates has come to concern many at large. Parents tend to be nurturing teachers of themselves with the pride of being mature decision-makers for the family. Still, their inception towards school leverage counts to promote the communication expertise to showcase excellence. The periodic motion of my child or my ward from the teacher to the parent comes with an ease of perception to a bit of gap.

At odd time intervals, the connection is a miss that preludes the children's success both in terms of knowledge seeker to the skilful attributes of concern. The lamination, which reserves because of this, has to explore with the empowered and enhanced parent-teacher communication expertise on cards and has a frequent occurrence in particular—believing that the parent's involvement activates the learning in a big way. To the density of understanding, this involvement caters to the supreme and impacts the outcome of the school education in totality. Bridging this gap is a universally accepted desire for now. The kids who engage themselves among peers to explore learning tend to deliver and count on the self-

learning mode of creative learners and information creation individuals. The database of the knowledge source ware activates their presence of deem interest to the peers. The parent's connection hence-forth is a priority as of now, and the following ideas and points tend to discover the universality of its acceptance:

School Diary/ Almanac, to some extent, delivers the freedom to share in writing with acknowledgement and share. This is one of the bonds which promote a connection.

With pride and pleasure of many, the Cloud-based Connect has mainly paved a new dimension and the definition of connecting with the stakeholders via the word of clue "ERP", which provides a platform which can integrate into the existing pedagogy and frees the teachers/ educators of connect and to make them perform better at their destined assignments.

We want to connect, as we, the parents, confirm the engagement in our children's school's education as an observer, the communication and the connection, in particular, the limiting belief towards the students by the teachers. The teachers do have, but the limited time in the classroom with the classroom sizes not paving a fixed number makes it impossible to identify the concept of understanding for every student in the school itself. No wonder the power of technology has paved a proper instant communication methodology; the limitations preview a different mindset. Without changing how the classroom is taught, there is no way to identify learning levels and customise and distribute content based on those learning levels. The tech candies dwell here with perception and dilute the masses' tension in most the unique ways.

With the advancement, the parents can connect and continuously engage in their child's learning and development through the automated reports, letting them know what was taught in the class, their child's learning levels, and how they have been progressing in particular. The aimed requisite is to communicate, collate and collaborate in conjunction to deliver the best for the stakeholders, the ultimate google generation of the day, who pact to learn at their leisure and pleasure without the chalk or duster but at the pace of their interest via the communication tool of theirs at prosperity. The ultimate is the spectrum to deliver engagement for the masses within the rooms of knowledge show and

cyberspace, gaining the repute of ORM, the Online Reputation Management for the educators at large. This is a particular fact of soliciting culture to dwell and explore the narration.

The taste of technology has yielded a pace with the march to deviate many schools to come on apps to the surprise of many, which offers a detailed lookout of connecting with base.

I remember the fantastic fable here about the High-Flying Balloons: A man was selling balloons on the streets of New York City. He knew how to attract a crowd before offering his wares for sale. He took a white balloon, filled it up, and let it float upward. Next, he filled a red balloon and released it. Then he added a yellow one. The little children gathered around to buy his balloons as the red, yellow, and white balloons were floating above his head. A hesitant boy looked up at the balloons and finally asked, "If you filled a black balloon, would it go up too?'. The man looked down and said, 'Why, sure! It's not the colour of the balloon; it's what's inside what makes it go up!'

What's inside of you determines whether you achieve peak success experience in your life. Climbing to the peak depends upon your mind and your attitudes.

The learning from the above comes as an essence to motivating our students, being attracted to positive comments, and being ready to excel in life like the high balloons with no colour of choice but the high expectations in particular. Let sky maybe not be the limits towards success, for it counts to be a Kaizen as a habit rather than an occasional occurrence. For today the teachers need to connect at length to the parents and the students with equal pace and density of satisfaction to pave their being STREET SMART! with the very connect of doses and learnings of fertilised future of their wards in particular. As for teachers, anger at times is a preface of irritation within the classroom situations. Let there be a niche of the tale, "Kill Anger before it kills you !" we at times blame different things for losing our temper, let this be off the routine if there has to be a win-win situation for all, for children will only like the subject if they like the TEACHER!

Happy Teaching and Parenting too!

About The Author

www.authordheerajmehrotra.com

Dheeraj Mehrotra has been honoured with the President of India's National Teacher Award in the year 2006 and the Best Science Teacher State Award, Innovation in Education for his inception of Six Sigma In Education by Education Watch, New Delhi and Education World- Best Teacher Award, BOLT Learner Teacher Award by Air India, 'Innovation in Education Award 2016' among others. He has developed over 150 FREE EDUCATIONAL MOBILE Apps for the Google Play Store exclusively for Teachers, Students, and Parents. This work has been recognized by the LIMCA BOOK OF RECORDS & INDIA BOOK OF RECORDS as the only Indian to draw that feast. Dr Mehrotra is presently working as a PRINCIPAL at KUNWARS GLOBAL SCHOOL, Lucknow, in India. He is an active TEDx speaker. As a premium UDEMY Instructor, he has also developed over 450 courses and is catering to over 8 Lakh students from 180 plus countries.

He can be visited at

www.authordheerajmehrotra.com

Books By The Same Author

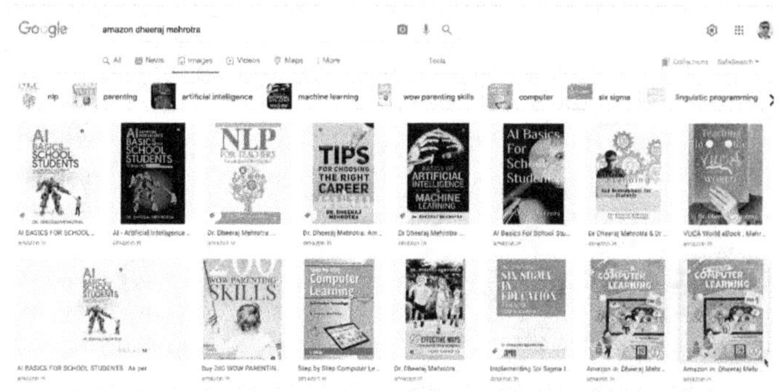

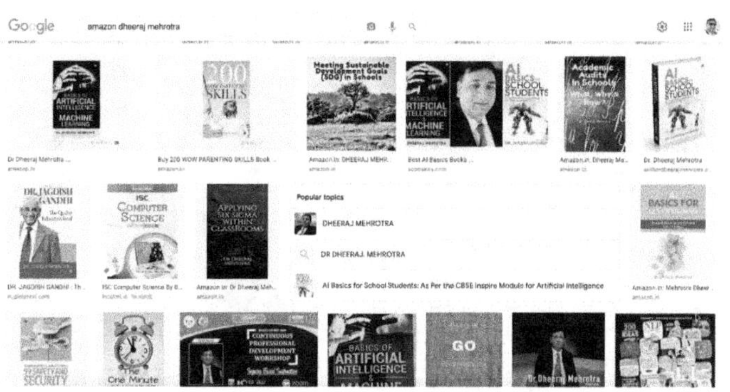

For more details visit:
www.authordheerajmehrotra.com